A PRACTICAL GUIDE
FOR SYSTEMS AND
PHONE REPAIRS

The Repairers and non-repairers book for fixing, sorting and servicing procedures

Sterling H. Kelvin

Table of Contents

CHAPTER ONE

INTRODUCTION

There are simple and easy methods to repair your devices which are outline and extensive describe along; from standing point inversion to ending intercession.

THE INVESTIGATING METHOD IN MOBILE DEVICE FIXING

USING VERSATILE WORKING VOLTAGE

Knowing the working voltage of a cell phone is vital.

Compassionately observe it as it is the initial step of the analysis of any cell phone for shortcoming. The Versatile Battery Voltage MBV ought to be between 3.7V to 4.2V. On the off chance that the battery is underneath the given reach, the cell phone won't work.

In this situation, you really want to help the battery through DC Power Supply or Battery Sponsor so it arrives at above 3.7V.

MOBILE FINDING STRATEGIES

Cold Testing Strategy

Cold testing is the point at which we utilize a multimeter to really look at the worth of obstruction at the hour of fixing a shortcoming in a cell phone. During cold testing don't drive the telephone from any gear. Utilize the diode reach and blare sound from the multimeter to pick apart the cell phone.

Hot Testing Strategy

The Hot testing strategy is embraced when the shortcoming can't be found or when the cell can't be fixed utilizing the virus testing technique. In this technique, the voltage of the harmed part or part is checked.

The shortcoming is found by fueling the cell phone with a battery or with the DC power supply. When you power the telephone, you ought to associate the Dark test of the Multimeter to the ground of the telephone's PCB and guarantee the red Test contacts the Testing Focuses.

CHAPTER TWO

INTERSECTION IN REPAIRING

HOW TO DIAGNOSING ISSUE UTILIZING DC POWER SUPPLY

Basic one

If DC Amp is fluctuating between .15 to .75 Amps and moving to no once the power on button is left, then it very well may be a Power IC Issue.

Basic two

If DC Amp is fluctuating between .10 to .20 Amps and moving to No once the power on button is left, then, at that point, it very well may be a product issue. Reboot or glimmering might determine the issue, in the event that not really looks at Power IC central processor.

Basic three

If there is no development of the Ampere Needle of the Power Supply, then the Battery connector, ON or OFF Switch Track, RTC, or Organization Gem is harmed. Give intensity to these parts utilizing a hot air blower. In the event that the issue isn't addressed then check by supplanting them individually.

Basic four

If the Ampere Needle vacillates under 2 then there could be issues with programming or RTC Continuous Clock. If the Ampere needle remains at some proper point then there is an issue with the Blaze IC. If there is a signal sound from the DC Power Supply then there is an issue with + and - or the versatile handset is short.

ESSENTIAL APPARATUSES TO FIX PHONE WIRELESS

Battery Promoter

A battery promoter is utilized to support the force of battery of a cell phone.

Battery Analyzer

This gadget is utilized to test and dissect status or state of battery of a portable mobile phone.

Multimeter

A multimeter can be simple or computerized. In cell phone fixing, generally a computerized multimeter is utilized to find flaws, really look at track and parts.

Welding Iron

A welding iron is utilized to patch little parts like capacitor, resistor, diode, semiconductor, controller, speaker, receiver, show and so on. A 50 watt binding iron is sufficient for most cell phone fixing position.

PCB Holder PCB Stand

A PCB Printed Circuit Board holder or PCB stand is utilized to hold various sorts of PCB of a cell phone while binding or fixing.

Weld Wire

Test Dance Box

This gadget is utilized to analyze and track down shortcoming or issue in a cell phone. It assists the cell phone with working and capability typically outside its case or lodging

Cleaning Wipe

This is utilized to clean tip of patching iron while binding

LCD Analyzer

IRDA or Infrared Workstation

This machine is like hot air blower. Just contrast is that it gives heat through infrared. It is exceptionally exact and gives heat just where it is required consequently forestalling any harm to local electronic parts on a PCB.

Magnifying lens or Magnifier

These used to see an amplified perspective on PCB or electronic parts.

Antistatic Mat (ESD Mat)

An ESD Mat or Antistatic Mat is laid or put on the table or workbench where portable fixing is finished.

Hot Air Blower

A hot air blower is likewise called SMD Surface Mount Gadget revamp station and SMD fix framework.

Cell Phone Fixing Toolbox

Accuracy Screwdriver

Amplifying Light

Seeing the amplified perspective on the PCB of a cell phone is utilized.

Screwdriver Pack

A screwdriver pack has a few screwdrivers of various shapes and sizes to disguise and gather a cell phone.

Tweezers

Tweezers are expected to hold electronic parts, ICs, jumper wire and so forth while patching and Desoldering.

DC Power Supply

Controlled DC Direct Current power supply is utilized to supply DC current to a cell phone.

Jumper Wire

Jumper wire is a dainty overlaid or covered copper wire used to jumper starting with one point then onto the next on the track of a cell phone while fixing.

Patch Glue

Edge Shaper

This is utilized to eliminate cover from jumper wire.

Point Shaper

HOW TO USE A MULTIMETER IN CELL PHONE FIXES AND EASY ACCESS IN PROCESS

Basic one

DC Volt Setting; utilize this setting to actually take a look at the voltages of what to be checked. In DC volt setting the result voltage of different things like battery, battery connector, charger, charging connector, and so forth can be checked. It is demonstrated by a capital V and straight line with 3 dabs underneath it.

Basic two

Obstruction Setting; by this meter, the opposition of different parts like resistors, and so on can be checked. Can likewise look at obstruction between 2 focuses in event that is told to actually take a look at in a help manual to look at it to get a specific perusing while at the same time fixing a shortcoming in the motherboard; can likewise check the receiver of mobile phone with this setting,

Diode setting

At the point when you contact the red and the dark test closes while on this setting, you will actually want to hear a blare sound. By keeping the multimeter on this setting, we can actually look at the progression between the given 2 focuses. Can check regardless of whether the tracks are open.

On the off chance that the multimeter shows coherence, it will give a blare sound. That will imply that the track is alright. What's more, on the off chance that it doesn't blare, it will imply that the track is broken.

How to fix a messed up track

Jumpering implies fastening a flimsy protected wire from one finish of a wrecked track to the opposite end. With this setting, we likewise check regardless of whether the circuit board is short. Really look at the shorting by keeping the wires on the positive and adverse terminals of the battery connector and furthermore switch the wires.

In the event that get signal sound the two different ways, the circuit board is short, on the off chance that get blare sound just a single time, it isn't short.

CHAPTER THREE

INSTALLING AND FIXING FROM EXTERNALS

METHOD TO FIX A WATER HARMED CELL PHONE

First stage

Remove the battery right away; if at any point a telephone has been wet we and our eager brain tend to restart it to see whether it works once more or restarts, simply remember it that you never do this since it might seriously harm the circuit and it might interfere with you fiscally. Just let it stay off and the above all else step is to take out or withdraw the battery from the telephone. No power no mischief to your hardware. It is likewise better to eliminate the SIM cards from your handset, with the goal that the SIM put away contacts are flawless.

Second stage

Open and dry the whole stuff; so the following stage is to dry your cell phone without anyone else. Eliminate the front and back fronts of the telephone and blow warm air from your hairdryer and in a general movement all around your telephone in such a way that you work on the spots where you might figure water drops might have stopped up for example between bunched parts, mic, charging point, and so forth. After you feel guaranteed that water might have dried totally then you can again collect and cautiously switch on the handset. Make sure to utilize your dryer on a warm setting. Try not to utilize it on hot or, more than likely you might harm or dissolve any interior plastic parts. You can likewise dry all the stuff over a warmer or in direct daylight.

Third stage

Using an air blower, Blow medium air into the telephone to blow dry any water out of your telephone for this reason it need not be important to utilize an air blower you might utilize the blower of your homegrown vacuum cleaner too. After this you can cautiously turn on the handset.

Fourth stage

Other Regular strategy, you can likewise totally cover your handset with crude and uncooked rice for at some point say regarding six to eight hours with persistence so that water is retained totally by this technique. Rather than rice, silica granules are likewise one more powerful answer for drying water from your telephone. Yet, this isn't practical assuming your handset was totally splashed or soaked in water or water-logged.

PHONE HAVING KEY ISSUE AND SOLUTIONS TO IT

REMOVE KEY FROM LINK

In the event that you don't have an unkeyed link accessible, you might have the option to eliminate the key from the current link. Most keyed links utilize a little piece of plastic to obstruct one of the openings. You might have the option to utilize a needle to pry the block out far enough that you can remove it with your needle-nose forceps.

On the other hand, take a stab at driving a pin into the block at a point, then bowing the highest point of the pin over and hauling both twisted pin and block out with your forceps. On the off chance that the key is a strong, fundamental piece of the link which is seldom the situation, you might have the option to utilize a warmed needle or pin to soften the critical into a more healthy place far enough for the pin to situate.

REMOVE THE CULPABLE PIN

On the off chance that the stores are shut, the main link you have utilizes pin opening keying with a strong block that you can't get out, and you should interface that link to a header-pin connector that has all pins present, you need to go with what you have.

Basement pin off

You can utilize slanting cutters to nip off the pin that keeps you from interfacing the link. Clearly, this is extreme. Assuming you nip some unacceptable pin, you'll annihilate the motherboard or development card, or if nothing else renders that interface unusable. Before you cut, check whether you can trade links inside the PC to think of an unkeyed link for the issue connector.

Cut connector

If not, you can at times twist the culpable pin somewhat to the point of permitting the female connector to situate to some degree. This might be sufficient to use as an impermanent association until you can supplant the link. As a last resort and you really want to cut the pin, prior to doing as such, adjust the keyed female connector to the pin cluster and check just which pin should be cut.

HOW TO INSTALLED CARD IN COMPUTER

Eliminate the cover from the suspension and analyze the motherboard to figure out which development openings are free. Find a free extension opening of the sort expected by the development card.

Late computers might have a few sorts of extension spaces accessible, including 32-and 64-digit PCI universally useful development openings, an AGP video card space, a couple of PCI Express x16 video card spaces, and at least one PCI Express x1 highlight openings. Assuming more than one opening of the legitimate kind is free; you can lessen the probability of intensity related issues by picking one that keeps up with dividing between the extensions cards as opposed to one that groups the cards.

Openings

An access opening for every extension space is available on the back of the undercarriage. For vacant openings, this opening is impeded by a slight metal space cover got by a screw that strings descending into the frame. Figure out which space cover relates to the opening you picked. This may not be essentially as simple as it sounds.

Spacing

A few kinds of extension spaces are counterbalanced, and the opening cover that seems to agree with that opening may not be the right one. You can check which opening cover compares to a space by adjusting the development card itself to the space and seeing which space cover the card section matches to.

Screw and inwards

Remove the screw that gets the opening cover, slide the space cover out, and place it and the screw to the side. If an inward link blocks admittance to the opening, delicately shift it to the side or disengage it briefly, noticing the appropriate associations so you will know where to reconnect it.

Opposite and slide

Guide the development card delicately into position, however don't yet situate it. Confirm outwardly that the tongue on the lower part of the development card section will slide into the matching hole in the body and that the extension card transport connector segment adjusts appropriately with the development opening.

Twist and adjust

With an excellent case, everything ought to adjust appropriately with no work. With a modest case, you might need to utilize pincers to twist the card section somewhat to make the card, undercarriage, and space all line up. As opposed to doing that, we like to supplant the case. When you are certain that everything is appropriately adjusted, position your thumbs on the top edge of the card, with one thumb at each finish of the extension opening beneath the card, and press delicately straight down on the highest point of the card until it seats in the space. Apply pressure fixated on the extension space underneath the card, and abstain from curving or twisting the card.

Frame attachment

A few cards seat effectively with minimal material input. Others require a considerable amount of tension and you can feel them fit properly. When you complete this step, the extension card section ought to adjust appropriately with the screw opening in the frame. Replace the screw that gets the extension card section, and supplant any links that you briefly detached while introducing the card.

Turn on and check

Interface any outer links expected by the new card don't fix the thumbscrews yet and surrender the framework a fast once to ensure you haven't neglected to do anything. Turn on the PC and check that the new card is perceived and that it capabilities true to form. Whenever you have done as such, power the framework down, supplant the cover, and reconnect everything. Store the unused opening cover with your extras.

HOW TO UNINSTALLED EXTENSION CARD

Eliminate

Remove the framework cover and find the development card to be eliminated. It's astounding that it is so natural to eliminate some unacceptable card if you don't watch out. No big surprise specialists sporadically fail to understand the situation. Once you're certain you've found the right card, disengage any outer links associated with it. In the event that the card has interior links associated, disengage those too. You may likewise have to detach or reroute other inconsequential links briefly to get to the card.

Spot secure

Assuming this is the case, name those you separate. Remove the screw that gets the card section, and spot it securely aside. Grasp the card solidly close to the two closures and pull straight up with moderate power. On the off chance that the card won't deliver delicately rock it from front to back line up with the opening connector to break the association.

Weigh lightly

Be cautious while getting a handle on the card. A few cards have sharp weld focuses that can cut you gravely on the off chance that you don't play it safe. In the event that there's no protected spot to get a handle on the card and you don't have a couple of weighty gloves helpful, take a stab at utilizing weighty folded cardboard between the card and your skin.

Circle from form

If you intend to save the card, place it in an antistatic pack for capacity. It's really smart to name the pack with the date and the make and model of the card for future reference.

Wind current

On the off chance that you have a driver circle, toss that taken care of too. In the event that you are not introducing another development card in the cleared opening, introduce a space cover to guarantee legitimate wind current and supplant the screw that gets the space cover.